The # 2 of 3 Novelet
gel...

By: Joe D Tippens

The Unfinished Masterpieces

Chapter 1: The Great Unveiling

The first Saturday in October always brought a crisp bite to the air in Cresthaven, Colorado—the kind that made the aspen leaves shiver gold and tourists flock to the town's expensive galleries for "authentic mountain art." This year, the Voss family home—a sprawling, eccentric Victorian perched on a ridge overlooking the valley—looked like a mad architect's fever dream: turrets twisting like question marks, hidden skylights winking from unexpected angles, and enough secret passages to make a minotaur jealous and a building inspector weep. The house had been Elias Voss's playground, a labyrinth of creativity where every room hid a surprise, and every surprise hid a story—often one involving explosions, floods, or at least a minor electrical fire.

Clara Voss, sixty-eight and still sharp as a palette knife honed through decades of marital mayhem, stood in the grand foyer, surveying the chaos of Leonardo's Legacy Weekend preparations. Banners reading "Celebrating Elias Voss: Genius, Artist, Inventor Extraordinaire" hung crookedly from the rafters, one end dangling as if trying to escape the madness and elope with the chandelier. Caterers wrestled with trays of artisanal charcuterie that looked suspiciously like gas station jerky arranged in the shape of the Mona Lisa—complete with a cheese moustache already melting under the heat lamps. A string quartet warmed up in the corner, sawing out a wobbly version of "Flight of the Bumblebee" because Elias had once claimed it was "the soundtrack to invention," though Clara suspected he'd just liked how it annoyed the neighbors.

Clara raised an eyebrow, her wit as dry as the high-altitude air that made tourists gasp for breath. "You're three hours late, Julian. The caterers are out of brie, the quartet just switched to 'Sweet Caroline' because the cellist claims it's avant-garde, and the only critic fainting is the violinist—from last night's open bar. If you're looking for ecstasy, try the espresso machine. It's the only thing in this house that hasn't malfunctioned yet."

Julian waved a dismissive hand, nearly knocking over the easel again and causing the chicken-clock sketch to flutter like a panicked bird. "Details, Mother. Mere footnotes in the epic saga of Voss! Now, where's the new discovery? The rumor mill in New York is churning—saying you found something big, something that'll make the Met weep with envy and the Guggenheim beg for scraps."

Before Clara could respond, the door flung open again, slamming into Julian's suitcase and sending it gliding across the marble floor like a hockey puck on ice. Beatrice "Bea" Voss strode in, her power suit as sharp as a fresh banknote, briefcase swinging like a weapon in a boardroom battle. She kissed Clara on the cheek with the efficiency of a hostile takeover, then shot Julian a look that could curdle milk or melt steel—depending on her mood. "Traffic was murder. Tell me we're not auctioning anything yet. I need to review IP implications, tax ramifications, and whether that goat is deductible as a dependent or just a bad taxidermy investment."

Julian recovered his suitcase with a flourish, spinning it like a dance partner. "Bea, darling sister, always the bean-counter in a sea of dreams. Father's genius isn't for spreadsheets—it's for sonnets, symphonies, and at least one sonata played on a self-invented instrument that sounds like a cat in a blender!"

Bea rolled her eyes so hard that Clara worried she'd strain an optic nerve. "And your genius is for sonnets about unpaid rent and symphonies of excuses, Julian. Let's stick to facts: Dad's works could fund a small country if we play it right—or bankrupt us if we don't."

Theo ambled in behind her, carrying a ring light, tripod, and a GoPro already recording, his casual slouch a deliberate contrast to his siblings' high-energy vibe. "Hey, fam! Live streaming the homecoming for the channel. Subscribers are eating up the 'grieving genius' arc. We hit fifty thousand views on the teaser alone—'Elias Voss: The Man Who Invented Tomorrow, Yesterday.' Comments are fire: 'Can't wait for the family drama!'"

Clara pinched the bridge of her nose, her voice a mix of exasperation and affection formed from years of mediating Voss sibling disputes. "It's been six months since your father died, Theo. Can we grieve without a ring light? Or at least without turning it into a reality show complete with product placements and sponsor shoutouts?"

Theo grinned, undeterred, adjusting the ring light like a pro. "Content waits for no one, Mom. Besides, Dad would've loved the exposure. He once said, 'If a tree falls in a forest and no one films it, was it even art? Or just firewood for the uninspired?' I'm just honoring his wisdom—one viral clip at a time."

The grandkids tumbled in next: Lila with purple-streaked hair and a sketchbook held like a shield against the world's dullness, Milo dragging a mysterious duffel that clanked ominously, as if it contained a small arsenal of half-finished gadgets or maybe a portable junkyard, and Harper clutching a wind chime made from old paintbrushes that jingled like ghostly applause each time she bounced on her toes with boundless energy.

"Grandma!" Harper yelled, nearly knocking over Theo in her excitement and causing his tripod to wobble like a tipsy giraffe. "The chimes said Grandpa's excited today! They jingled extra loud when we pulled up—like he's throwing a party in the afterlife with da Vinci as the DJ!"

Clara smiled despite herself, kneeling to hug Harper and steady the tripod in one smooth motion. "Let's hope he's excited enough to keep the house standing, sweetheart. Last year's unveiling involved a minor fire—courtesy of Uncle Julian's 'dramatic lighting' that turned out to be a short-circuiting spotlight."

Julian dramatically clutching his chest, staggered back as if hurt. "It was ambiance! Mood! Not arson! The flames were symbolic—representing the burning passion of artistic pursuit!"

Bea snorted, crossing her arms. "Symbolic flames that cost us two thousand in smoke damage and a visit from the fire marshal. Let's not repeat that masterpiece, unless you're volunteering to explain it to the insurance adjuster again."

The plan for the weekend was simple on paper: unveil one newly discovered Elias Voss piece each day, culminating in a grand reveal Sunday night. Clara had spent months cataloging the accessible studios, but whispers among the town's art crowd hinted at more—hidden caches Elias had bragged about in his manic phases but never shown anyone. He'd been a true polymath, blending art and invention like da Vinci himself: paintings that moved with hidden mechanisms, sculptures that generated electricity, all born from the highs and lows of his bipolar mind. The highs were electric ideas flowing like rivers in flood. The lows were silent voids, where he'd retreat to the storm shelter or the bunker, emerging weeks later with raw, haunting works that spoke of inner turmoil.

Today's reveal: a sculpture called The Thinker's Revenge, supposedly hidden behind a false panel in the library.

Clara led the parade—family, caterers, quartet, and a dozen early-arriving guests—into the mahogany-paneled library. Bookshelves soared two stories high, reachable only by a rolling ladder Elias had rigged with a counterweight system involving bowling balls, pulleys, and what he called "da Vinci's pulley principles reborn for the modern klutz."

Julian dramatically stepped in front of the panel, his cape swirling as if he were about to summon a spirit from the art ether. "Allow me—the artistic son—to do the honors. Father would want it this way— with flair, with panache, with at least one close-up for Theo's channel."

Bea crossed her arms and tapped her foot. "Father would want it insured first. Don't break anything we can't deduct, Julian. Remember the 'kinetic sculpture incident' of 2015?"

Julian waved her off. "Pish-posh! That was a minor kinetic malfunction. The cat eventually recovered its fur."

Theo zoomed in with the GoPro. "And… action! This is where the magic happens—or the mayhem. Place your bets, chat."
Julian pressed the hidden latch with flourish. "Behold!"

Nothing happened.

He pressed harder, grunting like a weightlifter at the Olympics. "The latch is… stuck. A test of strength! Of will!"

Milo piped up from the back, duffel clanking as he shifted. "Maybe it's the bowling-ball release. Grandpa said it jammed if you didn't align the pulleys first. It's like da Vinci's crane system, but with more bowling."
Julian, never one to read instructions (or listen to teenagers), yanked the ladder's counterweight rope

instead. "Force it open with physics! Da Vinci would approve—levers and all!"

The ladder shot across the room like a runaway freight train on steroids, with bowling balls tumbling from an overhead chute in a chaotic cascade that would make Rube Goldberg jealous. One ball clipped the violinist in the string quartet, causing him to yelp and switch mid-note to a screeching cat sound that could shatter glass or summon real cats. Another bounced off a guest's foot, prompting a shout of "My gout! My precious gout!" The third ricocheted into the caterer's tray, launching the charcuterie Mona Lisa into the air like a meaty frisbee, cheese moustache flying off like a bad toupee.

The false panel—triggered by the sudden weight shift—popped open with a theatrical pop that echoed like a champagne cork at a bad party.
Everyone leaned forward, holding their breath like they were about to witness the birth of a unicorn—or at least a really good tax deduction.

Inside was not a sculpture.

It was a pressurized canister rigged to a motion sensor, labeled in Elias's scrawl: "Revenge is Sweet (and Sticky). Caution: Impatience Activated."
A soft hiss filled the room.

Then—WHOOSH.

A geyser of vibrant neon-pink paint exploded outward, covering Julian from head to toe in what looked like radioactive Pepto-Bismol mixed with unicorn vomit. He sputtered, arms flailing like a pink windmill in a hurricane, cape now a soggy rag slapping against his legs like a wet towel fight.
The spray continued, bouncing off bookshelves with the aim of a tipsy billiards player, splattering the caterers' backup trays into abstract edible art that Jackson Pollock would envy, and finally hitting Theo's GoPro lens in a perfect pink bullseye that turned the screen into a rose-tinted filter.

A guest slipped on the slick floor, falling into a pile of charcuterie and bowling balls, shouting, "This is why I stick to digital art! No one gets bowled over by pixels!"

The violinist, dodging pink droplets like they were acid rain, hit a high note that shattered a nearby vase—adding ceramic shards to the mess, turning the floor into a crunchy pink minefield.
Silence settled, interrupted only by the drip-drip of paint, the violinist's muttered curses, and Harper's wind chimes ringing from the foyer like distant laughter from the great beyond.

Julian stood frozen, dripping, looking like a melted flamingo in a cape that now resembled a used mop. He blinked pink out of his eyes, then deadpanned, "I… I look like one of Father's postmodern experiments. 'Portrait of a Son in Humiliation.' Subtitle: 'The Pink Period.'"
Bea, miraculously only lightly speckled like a minimalist freckle painting, burst out laughing—real,

belly-deep guffaws that echoed through the library. "You do! And it's your best work yet! Move over, Picasso—here comes Pinkasso!"

Theo wiped his lens and whispered to the camera, "Okay, chat, this is the most viewed video we'll ever post. 'Pink Panic: Genius Strikes Back.' Bonus points if it trends as 'Voss Family Bath in Bubblegum.'"
Milo high-fived Lila through the pink haze. "Grandpa's traps are legend. Ten out of ten for execution—literally paint-by-numbers execution!"

Harper clapped her hands, pink splatters flying like confetti. "The chimes predicted color today! Pink means surprise party!"

Clara stepped forward, gently plucked a note from inside the now-empty canister as if she were used to her husband's posthumous pranks, and read aloud amid the chaos:
If you're reading this, someone lost patience. Congratulations—you've found the decoy. The real

masterpiece is elsewhere. Love, Elias. P.S. The paint washes out. Eventually. P.P.S. Julian, stop yanking ropes without thinking. It's a bad habit—like your taste in capes.

Julian groaned, then laughed—a genuine, self-deprecating bark that cut through the tension. "He knew I'd be the one to pull it. Touché, Father. Touché. And for the record, capes are timeless!"

Bea wiped a tear of laughter from her eye. "Timeless like your ability to turn every room into a disaster zone? We should patent that—'Julian's Chaos Generator.'"

Theo: "I'd buy stock. As long as it comes with a pink filter."

Clara's lips twitched—the first genuine smile all day. "Your father always said art should surprise. Consider us surprised. Now, who's helping clean? Or do I call the fire marshal for 'hazardous materials'?"

Julian struck a pose, paint dripping like performance art. "I volunteer as tribute! The Pink Prince of Cleanup!"

The room erupted in laughter—guests, caterers, quartet all joining in.
Outside, the aspens rustled as if Elias were chuckling from the branches, his polymath pranks alive and well, keeping his family on their toes—and in stitches.

The hunt—and the hilarity—had officially begun. But beneath the pink chaos, a quiet current flowed: Elias's traps weren't just jokes. They were invitations—to laugh, to connect, to remember him not as a distant genius but as a playful, loving father.

Chapter 2: The Ornithopter Debacle and the Aerial Screw Surprise

By Sunday morning, the Voss house looked like a crime scene investigated by clowns who had lost a paint fight. Pink footprints tracked across Persian rugs like abstract expressionist breadcrumbs leading nowhere useful. The charcuterie Mona Lisa had been declared "post-modern" by a tipsy guest and partially eaten, leaving only a meaty smile and a single olive eye staring accusingly from the tray.

Julian—still faintly magenta despite three showers, a turpentine scrub, and a desperate attempt with dish soap—had started wearing oversized sunglasses indoors "for the artistic mystique" and to hide the fact that his eyebrows were now permanently tinged bubble-gum pink, giving him a constant look of mild surprise.

Clara stood in the kitchen, armed with industrial cleaner, steel wool, a bucket of soapy water, and a grim determination that could have scrubbed the Rockies clean, one boulder at a time. "We have two more unveilings today," she announced to the assembled family over coffee strong enough to strip varnish off antique furniture. "Let's try not to trigger any more of your father's practical jokes. I'm manifesting calm. Positive thoughts only. No pink. No explosions. Just dignified discovery."

Theo, uploading overnight footage titled "Pink Paint Prank: Dad's Ghost Strikes First" (already at three million views and climbing faster than Elias's old perpetual-motion prototypes), grinned over his laptop like a kid who'd discovered the internet's candy store. "Too late, Mom. Chat's calling Julian 'Barbie's Existential Crisis' and 'The Pink Prince of Pretension.' The comments are gold—someone made a GIF of him flailing with the caption 'When Dad's trap hits different.'"

Julian swept in dramatically, sunglasses perched on his head like a crown of shame, cape (now tie-dyed pink from yesterday's deluge and resembling a used dish rag) billowing behind him like a defeated superhero who'd lost a fight with a cotton-candy machine. "Let them mock! Suffering is the crucible of genius. Father would approve of my new 'Blush Period.' It's very… vulnerable."

Bea, scrubbing her briefcase with the fury of a woman who bills by the hour and hates surprises, snorted so hard her coffee nearly shot out her nose. "Vulnerable? Julian, you look like a flamingo that lost a fight with a cotton candy machine at a pride parade. Father would approve—of laughing at you."

Lila and Milo snickered from the corner, where they were trying to salvage a paint-soaked sketchbook by laying out pages like evidence at a crime scene. Harper twirled her paintbrush wind chimes, which jingled happily despite the chaos. "The chimes say today's color is blue! Like the sky! Or maybe bruises from yesterday!"

Clara exchanged glances with the adults—part exhaustion, part affection, part "how did we survive this man for forty years?" The attic—Elias's forbidden "aerial laboratory"—had been sealed since his death. He'd claimed it held "ideas too dangerous for gravity," muttering about da Vinci's flying machines during manic highs and sketching wings in the margins of grocery lists.

But the riddle from yesterday's canister had hinted: "Look where man dreams of conquering the sky, but fear keeps him grounded."

The attic it was.

The family procession—now including the cellist from the string quartet, who had crashed on the couch after drinking too much "medicinal" wine and was soothing his hangover with black coffee—climbed the narrow staircase. Dust motes danced in rays of light from a skylight Elias had installed himself, boasting about "optimal northern exposure for flight calculations and dramatic brooding."

Julian, cape billowing as if he were auditioning for a Renaissance Faire tragedy, found the hidden door behind a false bookshelf titled "Books Elias Pretended to Read (Mostly Da Vinci Biographies)."

"Aha! The latch is... here?"

He pulled a cord labeled in Elias's elegant script: **"Do Not Pull Unless Ready to Fly (Seriously, Julian, I Mean It—Love, Dad)."**
Naturally, Julian pulled—hard.

A counterweight system—pure Leonardo da Vinci inspiration, with gears and pulleys reminiscent of da Vinci's aerial screw designs—whirred to life with startling energy. The door swung open, but the sudden release triggered a secondary mechanism: a giant net of silk parachutes (another da Vinci concept Elias had obsessively prototyped in various sizes) deployed from the ceiling like a colossal jellyfish waking up grumpy and ready for revenge.

The parachutes unfurled in a chaotic flood, trapping everyone in a tight cocoon of silk that faintly smelled of mothballs and old dreams.

Julian flailed dramatically, voice muffled. "I'm ensnared in Father's embrace! Or his laundry! Someone free the artistic soul!"

Bea, wrapped like a burrito with only her head free and looking like a very angry caterpillar, yelled, "This is why we have trust funds—for therapy after family weekends! And dry cleaning!"

Theo's GoPro captured it all from underneath a canopy: Milo swinging from a parachute cord like Tarzan on a sugar high, yelling "Wheeee! It's a silk jungle gym!" Lila posing dramatically even while tangled, "This is performance art—'Trapped in Legacy'!" Harper giggling as silk draped her like a princess gown, "I'm a parachute fairy!" and the cellist (still half-asleep and now fully regretting his life choices) mumbling, "Is this part of the gig? Because my contract said no aerial stunts."

Clara, ever practical and the only one who read Elias's old attic notes, found the release cord hidden in a Da Vinci-style knot and yanked it with authority. The parachutes collapsed in a heap, leaving everyone in a silk pile-on that looked like a failed magic trick performed by incompetent wizards.

When they finally freed themselves—Julian's cape now tightly knotted around his legs like a poorly tied toga, Bea's hair escaping its bun in unruly wisps, Theo's GoPro covered in dust bunnies—the attic revealed itself: a vast space filled with half-finished wonders that would make any museum curator weep with envy or fear.

In the center hung a full-scale model of an **ornithopter**—da Vinci's famous wing-flapping flying machine, but Elias had "improved" it with modern lightweight carbon-fiber frames, electric servo motors for precise wing movement, collapsible joints inspired by bird anatomy, and even a small lithium battery pack for assisted takeoff. The wings—spanning fifteen feet—were covered in translucent silk painted with detailed anatomical studies of bird muscles, feathers, and flight paths.

Julian gasped, sunglasses falling off his nose in awe. "It's... it's Leonardo's ornithopter! Father built a working prototype! Look at the servo articulation—pure genius! The battery integration solves da Vinci's power problem with 21st-century elegance!"

Milo rushed forward, eyes shining as if he'd found buried treasure. "And the collapsible mechanism is based on da Vinci's folding bridge designs! Patentable. Definitely patentable. I can already see the upgrades!"

Bea examined the wing joints with professional curiosity. "The weight distribution is revolutionary. This could inspire modern drone tech—or at least a very expensive art installation."

Theo leaned in reverently, voice hushed for once. "This could actually fly. Drone laws be damned—

content gold! 'Man Flies da Vinci's Dream—Live from Dad's Attic!'"

Clara's eyes misted, memories flooding back. Elias had spent years studying da Vinci, calling him "the original polymath who understood that art and engineering are lovers, not strangers." During manic highs, he'd work through the night on flight models, muttering about "conquering gravity with elegance," emerging with wild hair and sketches that looked like birds dreaming of being machines.

But the real surprise waited in the corner: a large helical rotor suspended from the ceiling—Elias's take on da Vinci's **aerial screw**, the conceptual precursor to the modern helicopter. Brass blades spiraled upward in a perfect double helix, attached to a pedal mechanism, a small electric booster motor, and counterweights for stability. The blades were etched with tiny Vitruvian figures, as if humans were part of the spiral.

Harper clapped, chimes jingling in approval. "It's a flying windmill! Grandpa's spirit machine! Look—the blades have little people dancing!"

Julian, undeterred by yesterday's pink humiliation and today's silk entanglement, climbed onto the seat with theatrical flair that would make a Shakespearean actor jealous. "If da Vinci dreamed it, Father perfected it. I shall test the aerial screw in his honor! For art! For science! For dramatic content and the vindication of my pink eyebrows!"

Clara reached out, voice sharp with maternal alarm. "Julian, no—remember the rope rule!"

Too late.

He pedaled furiously, cape flapping like a surrender flag in a hurricane. The rotor spun, producing surprising lift with a satisfying whir. The device rose... six inches.

Then the booster kicked in—overcharged from years of storage, capacitors swollen with pent-up energy like a prank waiting to unleash itself.

WHOOSH.

The aerial screw shot upward like a brass rocket fired from a circus cannon, slamming into the reinforced skylight (which Elias had bragged "could withstand a small meteor—or Julian's ego") with a gong-like CLANG that rattled the entire attic. The impact shook dust from the rafters in a glittery cascade (leftover from yesterday, apparently) and triggered the ornithopter's motion sensors—Elias's final, devilish joke.

The ornithopter's wings started flapping on their own, electric motors humming to life with a sound like a thousand furious hummingbirds. The massive structure lurched forward on its suspension rig, wings beating with startling force that sent gusts rushing through the attic.

Julian, still pedaling mid-air and now spinning like a top, yelped in a pitch that could summon dogs. "This is not flight! This is aerial assault! Father, you magnificent bastard!"

The flapping ornithopter toppled easels in a domino chain that would impress professional bowlers. Sketches scattered like confetti at a wild parade. Paint tubes—left uncapped from Elias's last manic session—burst on impact in rainbow splashes, splattering everyone with a fresh coat of color that made yesterday's pink seem subtle. Glitter (from Lila's secret art supplies hidden in the attic for "emergencies") mingled with dust and paint, forming a sparkling tornado that caught the sunlight in a prismatic chaos, turning the attic into a wild disco.

Bea ducked behind a workbench, yelling over the noise, "This is why we have liability insurance! And therapy funds!"

Theo, laughing maniacally while filming through the glitter storm, shouted, "This is the best episode yet! 'Da Vinci's Revenge—Live and Flapping!' Chat's gonna crash the servers!"

Milo tried to shut down the ornithopter's power switch but slipped on spilled paint, sliding across the floor like a human curling stone into Julian's dangling legs. Julian spun faster, cape wrapping around his head like a blindfold. "I can't see! But I feel the genius!"

Harper danced in the glitter-paint storm, arms wide. "It's snowing rainbows! Grandpa's happy party!"

Lila struck poses amid the chaos, paint-splattered and glorious. "This is performance art! Someone get Valentina on the phone—she'll pay millions for this installation!"

The aerial screw finally lost momentum, depositing Julian in a heap on a pile of silk parachutes—cape over his head, legs in the air, dignity somewhere in the rafters with the dust bunnies.

The ornithopter's wings slowed, then stopped, one feather-light flap at a time, as if bowing out.

The attic fell silent except for heavy breathing, dripping paint, the occasional clank of settling gears, and the distant jingle of Harper's chimes downstairs.

Julian emerged from the pile of parachutes, covered head to toe in paint, glitter, and feathers from a burst pillow that had joined the chaos. He looked like a wild peacock that had lost a fight with an explosion at a craft store and a rainbow.

He blinked, then burst into laughter—deep, healing belly laughs that echoed through the attic like Elias's own manic cackle.
I look like one of Father's failed experiments! 'Man Attempting Flight, Mid-Humiliation.' Subtitle: 'The Glitter Period.'

Bea, covered in paint but smiling wider than she has in years, helped him to his feet. "You do. And it's magnificent. Finally, some honest art from you."
Theo wiped his lens, still chuckling. "Twenty million views by dinner. Guaranteed. We're breaking the internet—again."

Lila high-fived Milo through the mess. "Grandpa: two. Us: zero. But what a way to lose!"

Harper placed a rubber anatomical eye (dislodged from yesterday's chaos) on the ornithopter's wing. "He's watching. And laughing."
Clara surveyed the wreckage—sketches scattered, inventions askew, family looking like survivors of a pride parade explosion crossed with a paint factory detonation—and laughed. Truly laughed, the kind that started in her belly and shook her whole body.

"Your father," she said, wiping tears of mirth, "always had a flair for the dramatic reveal. Even when it involved turning his children into living abstract art." Julian struck a pose—red-drenched, ridiculous, radiant.
"Touché, Father. Touché."

Outside, the wind picked up, rattling the cracked skylight as if Elias were applauding from the clouds, his polymath pranks keeping the family on their toes—and in stitches.

The weekend was far from over.
And the family—paint-smeared, glitter-coated, and completely lively—was closer than ever, united by laughter and the lingering echo of a genius who loved them enough to hide his legacy behind joy.

Chapter 3: The Vitruvian Vault and the Proportional Panic

Tuesday arrived with a deceptive calm in Cresthaven — the kind of clear mountain morning where the air smelled like pine and potential, and the only clouds were the fluffy, non-threatening ones drifting lazily across the pale blue sky. The Voss house, however, had never experienced a peaceful morning it couldn't turn into a three-ring circus, and today was no different.

Clara gathered the family in the dining room at nine sharp, armed with fresh coffee and the leather-bound journal from the attic. The mechanical heart model sat on the sideboard, still faintly pulsing under a protective glass dome Milo had put in place overnight "to keep it dreaming," although it now occasionally thumped ominously, making the silverware rattle.

"Today's clue," Clara announced, reading Elias's elegant, mirror-script note aloud:

Leonardo understood that man is the measure of all things. Find where I have measured myself against the universe. Proportion is essential—and so is patience. (Julian, I'm looking at you. Again.)

Julian, who had finally removed most of the glitter from his hair but now sported faint pink streaks like accidental war paint and a permanent squint from yesterday's aerial antics, snapped his fingers with theatrical flair. "Vitruvian Man! Father was obsessed with da Vinci's perfect proportions. There's a sealed chamber in the east turret—he called it the Proportion Vault. Or was it the Symmetry Sanctum? Something pompous."

Bea, scrolling through her tablet's valuation spreadsheet while sipping her third espresso, rolled her eyes so hard the sound was almost audible. "The one he locked after he installed that ridiculous rotating floor during the 'human centrifuge' phase? I thought we bricked it up after the incident with the bowling balls and the goat."

Theo, setting up a discreet tripod (he'd promised "tasteful B-roll only," but old habits die hard), grinned. "Chat's already placing bets on a human-sized hamster wheel versus a proportional catapult. Odds are 2:1 on something spinning us into oblivion."

Lila and Milo were halfway out the door, racing like it was Christmas morning. Harper skipped behind, wind chimes jingling like an excited alarm clock. "The chimes are singing in rounds today! Like canon music! Or a warning siren!"

Clara sighed the sigh of a woman who had survived forty years of Elias's surprises and was now surviving his posthumous ones. "Upstairs. And for the love of all that is holy, no yanking ropes, pulling cords, or pressing anything labeled 'Do Not.'"

The east turret—a narrow, circular tower Elias had converted into a private studio—was accessible only by a spiral staircase so tight that Julian's cape (still slightly damp and now smelling faintly of turpentine) kept snagging like a dramatic sail in a bottleneck.

At the top, a heavy oak door awaited, its surface etched with a faint outline of the Vitruvian Man—circle and square superimposed, but with subtle differences: arms slightly elongated, legs a bit shorter, measurements in Elias's own handwriting scrawled in the margins like sarcastic footnotes.

Bea traced the lines with professional interest. "These aren't standard Vitruvian ratios. Dad personalized them—his own body proportions, with notes on 'emotional symmetry' and 'the imbalance of genius.'"

Milo spotted small brass pins at the four extremities and center. "It's a physical combination lock! We have to pose like him to open it. Human key!"

Lila clapped. "I call torso! I've got the best posture."

What followed was forty-five minutes of pure, escalating Voss slapstick that would have made da Vinci himself question the proportions of human dignity.

Attempt One: Julian dramatically sprawled on the hallway floor in full Vitruvian pose—arms and legs spread to match the etching, cape fluttering like wings. "Behold! The Renaissance lives! In me!" Nothing.
Bea: "The Renaissance called. It wants its dignity back."

Attempt Two: They tried stacking—Harper on Milo's shoulders for height, Lila and Julian extending their arms sideways like a human cross. The structure wobbled dangerously.

Theo filmed. "This is either art or a lawsuit waiting to happen. Place your bets."

It collapsed into a heap of laughter, with Milo landing on Julian's cape and rolling both of them into a human burrito that collided with the forgotten cello case from the string quartet, causing it to slide down the stairs with a mournful twang.

Julian, muffled from inside the cape cocoon: "I'm trapped in my own symbolism! The cape has betrayed me!"

Attempt Three: Bea calculated precise measurements from the etching. "Dad was 6'1". Arm span 6'3". We need exact replication—accounting for shoe height and ego inflation."

They recruited the cellist (still lingering for leftover charcuterie and now regretting every life choice) as a stand-in for height. Julian and Theo stretched fishing line for alignment while Lila marked positions with painter's tape that kept sticking to everyone's shoes.

Harper, bored and impatient, pressed all five brass pins simultaneously while humming the Bumblebee tune.

Click.

The door swung inward silently.
Julian untangled himself triumphantly. "See? Childlike wonder triumphs over adult overthinking!"

Bea: "Or random button-mashing. Let's not award Nobel Prizes just yet."
The turret studio was breathtaking: circular walls, floor-to-ceiling, covered in interconnected Vitruvian studies—hundreds of sketches of the human figure in

circle and square, each variation incorporating family members.

Julian's dramatic arm span is rendered in bold charcoal. Bea's squared shoulders in precise ink. Theo's casual slouch captured mid-motion. Even toddler versions of the grandkids, chubby limbs reaching for stars.

At the center: a life-size bronze sculpture of Elias as the Vitruvian Man—limbs on concealed gears, adjustable to infinite proportions, the metal polished to a warm glow.

On the pedestal: "The measure of genius is not perfection, but the infinite variations of love. Adjust me to fit your family."

They stared, awed.

Julian—tears in his eyes despite his best efforts—moved the bronze arm to match his own dramatic reach.

Click.

A hidden drawer opened in the base.

Inside: the next codex, and a rolled canvas.

They unrolled it together on the floor.

A stunning painting: the entire family depicted as overlapping Vitruvian figures—circle and square intertwined, limbs linking in an endless chain. Elias in the center, arms outstretched, holding them all with gears for joints and hearts at their centers.

And beneath, his note:

"You are my proportions. My circle. My square. My everything. The flaws make the whole."

The room fell silent.

Then Harper whispered, "Look—the floor."

The rotating floor Elias had installed started to turn—slowly, majestically—revealing a spiral staircase descending beneath the turret.

A hidden lower level.

Julian's voice quivered with excitement. "There's more? Father, you magnificent show-off."
Clara's eyes widened. "He never showed me this. Said it was 'for emergencies only.'"
They descended cautiously.

The lower chamber was small, dimly lit by a single skylight shaft—and chaos waiting to happen.

It was Elias's emergency storm shelter studio: reinforced walls, emergency supplies, and—because this was Elias—a full array of paints, canvases, and a single, massive blank canvas on an easel rigged with hidden mechanisms.

But the real feature is a pressure-sensitive floor connected to an old weather station on the roof. Elias had designed it to "capture the storm's energy" for inspiration.

As they stepped in—seven people on a floor calibrated for one—the mechanisms activated.
The floor vibrated.
Hidden fans whirred to life, simulating wind.
Sprinklers (meant for "rain inspiration") misted the room.
And the easel—loaded with pre-primed tubes—began squeezing paint in rhythmic bursts, splattering the blank canvas in chaotic streaks.

But the overload from seven sets of feet sent it haywire.
Paint tubes burst like fireworks.
Fans roared into gale force.
Sprinklers turned to full shower.
The canvas spun on its easel, flinging paint in centrifugal arcs.

Julian slipped first, landing in a puddle of ultramarine blue. "It's a baptism! In pigment!"

Bea tried to turn off the weather station panel but activated more fans. "This is not inspiration—this is a car wash for idiots!"

Theo, laughing and filming, was splashed with alizarin crimson. "Chat would pay for this—'Voss Family Paint Storm—Exclusive!'"

Lila and Milo skated across the wet floor like it was an ice rink, crashing into supply shelves that showered brushes and charcoal.

Harper danced in the spray, chimes jingling wildly. "It's raining art! Grandpa's happy storm!"

Clara, dodging a flying tube of titanium white, found the master kill switch (labeled "For When the Storm Gets Too Real") and slammed it.

Everything stopped—fans dying, sprinklers dripping to silence, easel slowing to a halt.

The canvas—now a chaotic mix of swirling colors, footprints, handprints, and accidental splatters—hung dripping.
They stood soaked, paint-drenched, breathless.
Julian looked at the canvas, then the family—mirrors of each other in multicolored chaos.

"It's… us," he whispered. "The real proportions."
Bea laughed—wet, free. "Flawed. Fabulous. Finished by accident."
Theo capped his lens. "Some art isn't for views."
Clara touched the wet canvas, tears mixing with paint.
"He knew we'd overload it. Knew we'd make a mess."
Harper: "And the mess is beautiful."

The unexpected twist settled gently amid the drips.
The lower chamber wasn't just a shelter.
It was Elias's final canvas—blank, waiting for the family to paint their truth.
Together.
Imperfectly.

Perfectly.

Chapter 4: The Anatomical Attic and the Heartbeat Hijinks

Tuesday brought a deceptive calm to Cresthaven—the kind of crisp mountain morning where the air smelled like pine and possibility, and the only clouds were the fluffy, harmless kind. The Voss house, however, had never experienced a peaceful morning it couldn't turn into a complete farce.

Clara gathered the family in the kitchen right at eight-thirty, holding a fresh pot of coffee powerful enough to wake the dead and Elias's journal open to a new page.

"Today's clue," she announced, reading in her calm, no-nonsense voice that somehow still carried the weight of forty years of marital mayhem:

Leonardo dissected truth to find beauty underneath the skin. Follow the heartbeat to where I dissected myself—and sometimes lost my own. Bring towels.

Julian, mid-sip of orange juice, did a theatrical spit-take that sprayed across the table like a poorly aimed fountain. "Anatomy! Father's anatomical phase—he was obsessed with da Vinci's drawings of muscles, hearts, écorché figures. There's a sealed studio in the west attic—the one with the weird pulsing light he installed during that 'cardiac inspiration' mania in 2012."

Bea, already on her second espresso and third spreadsheet tab titled "Potential Medical Patent Windfall," rolled her eyes so forcefully that the sound was almost audible. "The one he locked after the 'Heartbeat Symphony' incident? Where he rigged a subwoofer to play actual heart rhythms and nearly gave the mailman a coronary? I still get flashbacks."

Theo, setting up his GoPro on a tripod with the reverence of a cinematographer preparing for an Oscar-winning disaster flick, grinned. "Chat's already placing bets on whether we find a real heart or just Dad's dramatic interpretation. Odds are 3:1 on exploding arteries. Someone just donated a hundred bucks for 'red paint round two.'"

Lila rolled her eyes so forcefully she almost saw her own brain. "Because nothing says family bonding like arterial spray."

Milo bounced on his toes, duffel clanking. "Do we get to poke it with sticks?"

Harper jingled her chimes hopefully. "The chimes are thumping today! Like a drum solo! Or a warning!" Clara sighed the sigh of a woman who had survived forty years of Elias's surprises and was now enduring his posthumous ones. "Upstairs. And for the love of all that is holy, no yanking ropes, pulling cords, pressing anything labeled 'Do Not,' or giving Milo sticks."

The west attic staircase was narrower than the east, with a door at the top that looked innocent enough—until you noticed the faint red glow pulsing from the seams like a nightclub for vampires with arrhythmia.

Julian struck a pose in front of it, cape (still slightly damp and smelling of turpentine) billowing dramatically. "Behold! The portal to Father's inner workings! I shall lead the charge!"

Bea: "You lead every charge straight into disaster. Step aside, Captain Pinkbeard." Theo zoomed in.

"Title card: 'Heartbeat or Heart Attack—You Decide.' Subtitle: 'Brought to you by bad decisions.'"

No visible handle—just a small brass plate shaped like a human heart, with a stethoscope-like tube dangling from it like an invitation to eavesdrop on the afterlife.

Harper pressed her ear to the tube first. "It's beating! Like a real heart—but faster. Like Grandpa after three espressos and a new idea!"
Sure enough, a rhythmic thump-thump sounded from inside—slow and steady, then quickening a bit, as if motivated by their presence. Or plotting.
Julian dramatically presses his ear, eyes closed in fake ecstasy. "It's Morse code! Or… no, it's syncing to my pulse. Father's genius lives! The heart recognizes its dramatic heir!"

Bea: "Or it's a motion sensor picking up your theatrical heartbeat, Julian. Calm down before you trigger a rave—or a 911 call."

Milo noticed tiny valves on the tube. "It's a biometric lock! We have to match the rhythm to Dad's resting heart rate. Like a drum solo password!"

Clara smiled softly, enjoying a rare honest moment. "Sixty-four beats per minute. He bragged about it constantly—'the rhythm of a true polymath, steady as a metronome, unlike my children's chaos.'"

They counted in unison—Julian conducting like an orchestra maestro, Bea tapping her foot with lawyer precision, Theo mouthing numbers for the camera.

The mechanism thumped at exactly sixty-four.

Julian twisted the brass heart valve to "64" with a flourish that would make a matador jealous.

Click.

The door swung inward on silent, well-oiled hinges—revealing a turret studio that was a masterpiece of controlled chaos.

Walls are hung with Elias's anatomical masterpieces—hundreds of drawings inspired by Leonardo da Vinci's legendary studies, but with Voss's unmistakable twists: écorché figures with hidden clockwork gears driving joint movement; hearts dissected in cross-section with valves replaced by tiny turbines and springs; a full-size torso where arteries carry vibrant paint instead of blood, flowing into brushes that "paint" veins on the paper.

In the center, on a rotating pedestal illuminated by a soft, pulsing red glow, stood Elias's masterpiece: a life-sized anatomical model of a human figure—made of wax, wood, and brass, with muscles carefully carved and painted—posed like da Vinci's Vitruvian Man, but with a transparent chest cavity revealing a mechanical heart that truly beat.

The heart was a marvel: brass chambers pumping red-tinted fluid through leather valves, driven by a hidden pendulum clock and subtle electric assist. Tubes ran to the limbs, making veins "pulse" under the wax skin in perfect rhythm—thump… thump… thump.

Harper whispered, awe-struck, "It's Grandpa's heartbeat. He put his own heart in it. Literally."

Lila traced a drawing of a hand—Elias's own, annotated with notes on brush grip, invention dexterity, and a sarcastic "Don't lose this one in a manic shopping spree."
Julian's voice cracked with genuine emotion beneath the drama. "He dissected his own genius. Literally. Look—the heart valves are labeled 'High,' 'Low,' and 'Love.' The man was a poet."

Theo circled slowly, filming with reverence for once. "This is… museum-level. The Tate Modern would kill for this. Or at least maim. Quietly."
Bea noticed a leather portfolio on a side table. Inside: patents—filed but never pursued—for a "biomimetic prosthetic heart pump" based on the model's design,

potentially revolutionary for medical technology. "This could save lives. He sat on it."

And beneath the patents, a letter addressed to the family in Elias's hand:

Leonardo drew what he saw beneath the skin to understand motion, life, beauty. I drew you—all of you—to understand the same. My heart beats in these walls, in your laughter, in your arguments, in the way you forgive me when I disappear into the storm. Don't sell the mechanism. Let it beat for those who need reminding they're alive—even when they feel mechanical. Love, E.

The mechanical heart gave an extra, almost playful thump—as if winking.
Then, because this was still the Voss house and Elias had a sense of humor sharper than a scalpel and twice as twisted, the pendulum clock—slightly overtightened from years of disuse and the house's

subtle vibrations from yesterday's attic antics—gave a suspicious sproing.

The heartbeat accelerated.
Fast.
Thump-thump-thump-thump-thump.

Julian: "Uh… is that normal? Or is Dad having a posthumous caffeine rush?"
Bea: "No. That's tachycardia. In a wax man. We should—"
The fluid pressure built. Tubes bulged like overinflated party balloons at a very bad birthday.

Milo: "It's gonna—"

A seam in the transparent chest split with a comical pop that sounded strangely like a whoopee cushion. Red fluid sprayed in a dramatic, fountain-like arc—directly onto Julian's freshly cleaned blazer, turning his "minimalist mourning chic" into a full-on crime-scene reenactment. He flailed, arms pinwheeling. "It's alive! And it hates my wardrobe!"

The spray ricocheted—hitting Theo's GoPro right in the center, turning the screen into a rose-colored horror filter. Theo yelped, "My lens! It's bleeding!"

Bea tried to dodge but slipped on the initial puddle, landing flat on her back in the growing red pool. "This is not in my contract! I bill by the hour, not by the arterial spray!"

The figure's arms—geared to the heartbeat—began flailing in mechanical panic, knocking over easels in a domino wave that sent sketches flying like anatomical confetti at a bizarre parade.

A tube whipped loose like an angry snake, hosing Lila and Milo in synchronized red bursts. Lila shrieked, "It's like Carrie's prom but with more science!"

Milo, laughing hysterically, tried to grab the tube and got yanked off his feet, sliding across the floor like a human Slip 'N Slide into a shelf of rubber anatomical models—hearts, lungs, eyes—that bounced around the room like grotesque pinballs.

One rubber heart bounced off Julian's head with a squeaky boing. "Ow! Even in death, you're throwing things at me, Father!"

Harper danced in the red mist, wind chimes jingling wildly like a demented ice-cream truck. "It's raining Grandpa's love! Red means passion!"

The flailing wax arms knocked over a tower of paint cans—uncapped, naturally—creating a secondary rainbow explosion that mixed with the red into a swirling, slippery mess.

Bea, now completely soaked, tried to stand but slipped again, landing in Julian's lap. "This is undignified! I went to Harvard for this?"

Julian, cradling her like a damsel in a terrible romance novel: "Fear not, sister! I shall shield you from the arterial assault—with my body!"

Theo, laughing so hard he could barely hold the camera steady: "This is the best episode yet! 'Anatomical Assault—Live and Pulsing!' Chat's donating just to watch us drown in Dad's feelings!"

Clara, dodging a flailing wax arm that nearly took her head off, reached the hidden kill switch (labeled, of course, "In Case of Cardiac Overenthusiasm—Pull Hard, Laugh Harder") and yanked it with both hands.

The heart slowed. Stopped. The figure froze mid-flail, one arm pointed accusingly at Julian like a wax statue of judgment.

Silence—broken only by dripping fluid, squeaking rubber organs settling, heavy breathing, and the distant jingle of Harper's chimes downstairs.

Julian, soaked head to toe in red, looked down at himself and burst out laughing—deep, healing belly laughs. "I look like I lost a fight with a ketchup factory. Again. Father, you are magnificent, malicious genius."

Bea, sitting in his lap and equally drenched, joined in despite herself—laughter bubbling up like the fluid from the tubes. "You do. And it's magnificent. I haven't laughed this hard since Dad's 'perpetual motion barbecue' exploded and singed the neighbor's cat."

Theo wiped his lens, still chuckling. "Thirty million views by dinner. Guaranteed. We're not just breaking the internet—we're dissecting it."

Lila high-fived Milo through the mess, both slipping and landing in a heap. "Grandpa: three. Us: zero. But what a way to lose!"

Harper placed a squeaky rubber heart on the pedestal. "He's happy. The chimes say so. They're laughing too."

Clara touched the now-still mechanical heart, voice soft amid the chaos.

"Your father always did have a flair for the dramatic reveal. Even when it involved turning his children into walking Jackson Pollocks."

Julian struck a pose—red-drenched, ridiculous, radiant.

"Touché, Father. Touché. And bravo."

Outside, the sun broke through the clouds, casting red-tinted rainbows across the wet windows—like Elias's final wink.

The hunt wasn't over.

But the family—paint-splattered, laughing, and utterly alive—was closer than ever, connected by the joyful, pulse-quickening truth of a man who loved them enough to make even his chaos feel like home.

Chapter 5: The Mirror Maze and the Reflections of Regret

Wednesday settled over Cresthaven like a soft, forgiving blanket—too soft, the kind that makes you suspicious in a house full of Elias Voss surprises. The mountains gleamed under a light dusting of snow, the air sharp with pine and the faint, lingering scent of turpentine from yesterday's anatomical spray-down.

After the heartbeat hijinks (Julian was still finding red fluid in odd places, like behind his ear and in his shoe), Clara declared a "no new studios" day. Instead, she herded everyone into the conservatory for what she called "a gentle activity—something reflective."

The conservatory—a glass-walled jungle of overgrown ferns, skylights, and climbing vines—housed Elias's infamous mirror maze: a spiral labyrinth of full-length mirrors framed in ornate brass, designed during one of his "optics and introspection" phases. He'd claimed it helped him "see himself from every angle—literally and figuratively."

Clara held up the latest journal page, discovered tucked behind the mechanical heart's final valve like a cardiac Easter egg.

"Today's clue," she said, voice calm but with that telltale edge that meant business. "No inventions. No explosions. Just reflection."

She read:

"Leonardo's mirrors reflected truth without judgment. Find where I reflected on my failures. The maze shows many paths, but only one leads forward. Bring tissues—and a sense of humor. P.S. Mona sends her regards."

Julian, mid-yoga stretch to "realign his proportions after yesterday's cardiac assault," snapped upright. "Mona? As in Lisa? Father's Mona Lisa obsession! He painted at least six versions—said the original's smile was 'the ultimate bipolar expression: happy, sad, and judging you all at once.'"

Bea, nursing coffee and a mild hangover from last night's "decompression" champagne, snorted. "He also said her smile was proof of alien involvement. Let's not take artistic license as gospel."

Theo, setting up a discreet handheld camera, grinned. "Chat's already theorizing hidden Mona Lisa. Someone donated fifty bucks for 'Mona Voss reveal.'"

Lila rolled her eyes. "Because nothing says therapy like going viral with a Renaissance meme." Milo bounced on his toes. "Do the mirrors do tricks? Like funhouse fat/thin ones? Or infinite Mona Lisas?" Harper jingled her chimes hopefully. "They're gonna show secrets! The chimes are whispering—and one sounds like a lady laughing!"

Clara opened the maze entrance—a simple arch with the inscription: "Enter at your own risk. Truth multiplies. So does embarrassment. And occasionally, smiles."

They stepped in single file.

At first, it was pure comedy gold—mirrors reflecting infinite Vosses in increasingly ridiculous configurations. Julian rounded the first corner and struck a pose. "Behold—infinite Julians! An army of genius ready to conquer the art world!"

His reflection army struck the pose back—then one mirror distorted slightly, making his nose comically elongated and his smile… enigmatic. Almost like… Julian recoiled. "Father! Even in death, you mock my profile with Mona Lisa's smirk?"

Bea turned a corner and found herself multiplied into a dozen power-suited versions. One mirror made her head tiny, body huge; another gave her Mona Lisa's mysterious half-smile. "Great. Now I look like my ego—and it's judging me."

Theo filmed his own reflection slouching infinitely, but one mirror superimposed Mona Lisa's eyes over his own. "It's like she's saying, 'Put the camera down, kid.' Creepy."

Lila struck artistic poses—her reflections fractured into a kaleidoscope of purple hair and dramatic eyeliner. One mirror gave her Mona Lisa's exact smile—knowing, amused, eternal. "Okay, this is cool—wait, why is one me smiling like I know all your secrets?"

Milo made monster faces; the mirrors stretched him into a beanpole, then squashed him into a meatball, and one added Mona Lisa's enigmatic grin to his goofy expression. "I'm the Mona Milo! Half monster, half masterpiece!"

Harper danced, chimes jingling in echo. "Look! Baby Harpers everywhere—and one has Mona's smile! She's winking!"

Clara smiled—until her reflection showed her younger self, exhausted, holding a manic Elias as he ranted about unfinished projects, with Mona Lisa's face superimposed over Clara's own—tired, loving, enigmatic.

The tone shifted.

The mirrors weren't just funhouse tricks. Elias had angled them with hidden two-way glass and subtle projectors—triggered by motion—to display old family photos and video snippets at precise moments, all framed with Mona Lisa's smile overlaying key faces.

Julian's next mirror: a loop of him at twenty-five, screaming at Elias during a manic episode—"You're hogging all the genius! There's none left for me!"—followed by Elias's quiet, hurt: "There's enough for all of us, son. You just have to find your own." Mona Lisa's smile overlaid Elias's face—knowing, sad.

Julian froze. "Oh. That one. With... her smile. Like she knew I'd regret it."

Bea's mirror: her at thirty, coldly telling Elias his inventions were "unmarketable hobbies" while refusing legal help. Elias's defeated slump. Her own tight smile—now replaced by Mona Lisa's enigmatic one, as if judging her past self.

Bea whispered, "I was such a bitch. And she's smiling like she saw it coming."

Theo's panel: teen him filming Elias during a low, mocking his "sad old man routine" for a school project. Elias's gentle: "One day you'll understand the difference between documenting life and living it." Mona Lisa's smile on Theo's young face—mocking his own mockery.

Theo lowered the camera. "Yeah. I get it now. And she's laughing at me."
Lila and Milo together: childhood arguments—Lila accusing Elias of favoring Milo's gadgets; Milo resenting the "next genius" label. Mona Lisa's smile on both their young faces—knowing, forgiving.

Lila: "We were kids fighting over scraps. And she's smiling like it was cute."

Milo: "Cute and stupid."

Harper's mirror: Elias holding toddler, her, whispering, "You don't have to be brilliant, little one. Just be kind." Then a later clip—Harper hiding during one of Elias's storms, scared. Mona Lisa's smile on Harper's face—brave despite fear.

Harper's lip trembled. "She's smiling because I was kind anyway."

Clara's turn: a private moment—her crying alone after a manic week, whispering to sleeping Elias, "I love your mind, but sometimes I miss my husband." Mona Lisa's smile overlaid Clara's younger, tired face—enigmatic, enduring. Clara's voice broke. "She's smiling because she knew I'd stay."

The maze came together in the center: a large, plain mirror.

They stood before it—seven Vosses, simply reflected.

But then—the twist.

The mirror rippled like water.
A hidden projector activated.
The reflection changed.

There, in the glass, appeared Elias—life-size, smiling Mona Lisa's exact enigmatic smile.
He spoke—recorded voice, warm and wry:
"If you're seeing this, you made it through the maze. Congratulations. You faced the reflections I was too scared to. Mona's smile? It's not happy or sad. It's knowing and knowing that love isn't in perfect proportions. It's imperfect people holding on.
I hid my failures because I thought you'd love the genius more than the man. But you loved the man—storms and all. Thank you.
The real masterpiece isn't behind you. It's in front of me—right now.

Keep smiling. Even when it's complicated.
Love, Dad."

The image faded.
The mirror showed only them again—tears, paint remnants, laughter starting.

Julian's voice cracked first. "He… he gave himself Mona's smile. The ultimate Dad joke."

Bea laughed through tears. "And it's perfect. Because he knew everything—and nothing."

Theo: "Some things aren't for views. This one's just… ours."
Lila: "He saw us fighting over his light when he was trying to share it."
Milo: "And we missed the parts where he was just… Dad."
Harper slipped her hand into Clara's. "He's proud of us. The chimes stopped whispering. They're smiling now."

Clara—tears falling freely—pulled them all into the center.

Julian: "Group hug in a mirror maze? Infinite awkward Vosses. Dad would approve."

Bea: "He'd probably rig the mirrors to spray us with glitter for emotional emphasis."

Theo: "Too late—we're already crying glitter from the attic."

They hugged—messy, laughing through sobs, reflections multiplying the moment into eternity.

Julian: "I spent years trying to be him. But he wanted us to be… better."

Bea: "We are. Because we stayed."

Theo: "And we're still here."

Lila: "Finishing what he started—together."

Milo: "Even if it means more explosions."

Harper: "Especially the explosions."

Clara held tight.

"He got his wish. We're seeing him. Really seeing him. And he's smiling—that damn Mona Lisa smile."

Laughter echoed through the maze—warm, healing, infinite.

Outside, the wind chimes sang a new melody—soft, harmonious, whole.

The maze had no exit.

But they'd found the way forward anyway—together, smiling like they knew the secret too.

Chapter 6: The Therapy Turbine and the Unspoken Currents

Thursday arrived with a restless mountain wind that rattled the Voss house windows like it was trying to get in on the family drama—and probably succeeding. After Wednesday's mirror-maze emotional avalanche (which had left everyone raw, teary, and oddly lighter), Clara made an executive decision over a breakfast of pancakes drowning in syrup and unresolved feelings.

"No more studios today," she announced, pouring coffee with the authority of a woman who'd survived forty years of Elias's surprises and was now surviving his posthumous therapy sessions. "We're doing something your father always dodged like a tax audit, a diet, or a serious conversation: actual therapy."

Julian, mid-bite of pancake, performed a theatrical spit-take, spraying syrup across the table like a poorly aimed fountain. "Therapy? Mother, are you suggesting we air our impeccably artistic laundry in front of a stranger? I prefer my emotional baggage hand-stitched and dramatically monogrammed."

Bea, wiping syrup off her laptop with a napkin and the fury of a woman who billed by the hour, smirked. "Your baggage is 90% capes and 10% ego, Julian. It could use some airing—and maybe a dry cleaner."

Theo, phone already in hand (he'd promised "no filming," but old habits die harder than Elias's pranks), grinned. "Chat's gonna lose it. 'Voss Family Therapy—Live Emotional Breakdown.' We'd break the internet. Again."

Clara slid a business card across the table like a poker ace hidden up her sleeve. "Dr. Elena Reyes. Art therapist in town. Specializes in creative families. Your father saw her once—in secret. Called her 'the only person who could dissect my mind without drawing blood.' I booked us a group session. Two hours. Non-negotiable. And Julian—no capes."

Julian clutched his chest like he'd been shot. "You wound me, Mother. Capes are emotional support garments. They billow when I'm vulnerable."
Bea: "They also billow when you're avoiding vulnerability. Like everything else."

Lila rolled her eyes. "Can we not turn therapy into content? For once? Some of us are still processing the mirror maze."

Milo: "What if the therapist makes us draw our feelings? I'm great at gears, terrible at feelings."

Harper jingled her chimes hopefully. "Maybe she'll let us paint our storms! Grandpa would like that—he said Mona Lisa's smile was the ultimate storm face."

Clara paused, a fond yet pained smile crossing her face. "Your grandfather's Mona Lisa obsession began in '85, during one of his best moments. He saw a reproduction in a magazine and became convinced her smile was the key to everything—bipolar mood, artistic genius, the meaning of life. He painted six versions over the years. The first one smiled when he was manic. The last one… well, it smiled when he was low, but sadder. Like she knew."

Julian: "He hung the third version in the foyer upside down for a month. Said it made her smile 'more honest.'"

Bea: "And the fourth one had gears behind the eyes. He claimed it blinked when no one was looking."

Theo: "I have footage of the fifth. The smile changes depending on the light. Dad swore it was alive."

Lila: "The sixth is still missing. He hid it during a low, said 'Mona knows too much.'"

Harper: "She's watching us now. The chimes say she's curious about therapy."

Clara stood, ending debate. "Car leaves in thirty minutes. Bring tissues. And Julian—no capes. Mona's smile is dramatic enough."

An hour later, they filed into Dr. Reyes's sunlit studio downtown: cozy chairs in a circle, abstract paintings on the walls that looked suspiciously like controlled chaos, and a small kinetic sculpture in the corner spinning lazily with air currents—like a therapy turbine measuring emotional wind speed.

Dr. Reyes—warm-eyed, unflappable, with a smile that said she'd heard every artistic excuse in the book—greeted them with herbal tea and zero side-eye.

"Clara filled me in on the week," she began. "Elias sounds like he was a force of nature. Bipolar genius often feels like living with a permanent creative hurricane—beautiful, destructive, impossible to predict. And from what I hear, he had quite the thing for Mona Lisa."

Julian sipped his tea suspiciously. "A 'thing'? Madam, it was a full-blown philosophical love affair. He called her 'the original enigmatic influencer.'"

Bea: "He also called her 'proof that women have been judging men since the Renaissance.'"

Theo: "He painted her with a speech bubble once that said, 'I've seen your browser history.'"

Dr. Reyes chuckled. "Sounds like he used her smile as a mirror for his own complexity. Let's try something. Draw your family as you experienced it growing up. No rules."

Scratch-scratch filled the room.

Julian drew Elias as a towering sun god with Mona Lisa's smile, family as tiny planets orbiting in awe/shadow.
Bea's was a precise org chart: Elias at the top with Mona's smile judging from a corner, arrows labeled "Inspire," "Disrupt," "Require Bailout."

Theo sketched a camera lens framing chaotic scenes—Elias mid-mania with Mona's smile overlaid like a filter.
Lila's was angry scribbles over a perfect circle with Mona's smile in the center, watching.

Milo drew interconnected gears with Mona's smile as the missing tooth.

Harper drew a large heart with lightning bolts, band-aids, and Mona's smile in the center.

Clara's house had many doors—some open, some locked, Elias visible at every window but always with Mona's mysterious smile.

Dr. Reyes let the silence linger, then spoke gently.

Genius like Elias's can feel like the sun—warm and brilliant. But standing too close burns; too far, you freeze. And Mona's smile? It's the perfect metaphor: always there, always watching, never fully explaining.

Julian's voice cracked first, trying for humor. "I worshipped him. Then hated him for being impossible to reach. Every time I tried to impress him, he was three ideas ahead—and Mona was smiling like 'Nice try, kid.'"

Bea laughed wetly. "I thought if I could protect his work—patents, money—I could protect us from the chaos. But Mona's smile in my drawing? It's saying, 'You missed the point, counselor.'"

Theo: "I hid behind the camera. Documented everything to feel close. But Mona's smile in my lens sketch? It's judging me for filming life instead of living it."

Lila: "I forged his style to feel seen. Thought if I could paint like him, I'd matter. But Mona's smile in my angry scribbles? It's gentle. Like 'You mattered anyway.'"

Milo: "I built things to prove I wasn't a disappointment. Mona's the missing gear—smiling like 'Stop trying so hard.'"

Harper: "I thought if I was perfect, the storms would stop. But Mona's smiling because I was kind even when I was scared."

Clara's tears fell freely. "I was his anchor. Managed the storms so he could create. But Mona's smile on my tired face? It's saying, 'You deserved to be seen too.' I never told him how lonely it got."

Dr. Reyes nodded. "That's the unspoken current. The highs electrify. The lows pull under. And Mona's smile—Elias's favorite mirror—reflects it all back without judgment. Just knowing."

Julian reached for Clara's hand, voice thick. "We're a mess, Doc. But we're our mess. Mona approved." Bea grabbed Theo's. "A patented, copyrighted mess—with emotional royalties." Theo linked with Lila and Milo. "With exclusive rights to the chaos—and the love." The grandkids piled in—until hands connected in a ridiculous, tangled circle.

Julian: "Group hug? In therapy? Dad would call this 'sentimental sabotage.' "Bea: "He'd also cry harder than us—and blame Mona for making him emotional." Theo: "Then invent a tear-powered turbine to harness it."

Lila: "Patent pending—by all of us."

Milo spun an imaginary gear. "With Mona's smile as the logo."
Harper: "The chimes approve. They're spinning happy."

Clara held tight, tears and laughter mixing.
"He'd hate the mushy stuff. But he'd love this part. And Mona? She's smiling widest of all."

Laughter broke through—messy, healing, loud enough to rattle the kinetic sculpture into a joyful whirl.

Dr. Reyes watched, smiling.
"Session over. But the work? That's just beginning."
They left lighter—still a mess, but a connected one, Mona Lisa's knowing smile echoing in their hearts.

Outside, the wind shifted—the turbine sculpture spinning faster, as if Elias and Mona were applauding together.

The weekend's final unveiling waited.
But whatever came next, they'd face it smiling—that enigmatic, loving, Voss-family smile.

Chapter 7: The Codex Closet and the Final Equation

Friday—the penultimate day of Leonardo's Legacy Weekend—dawned with a rare, perfect stillness over Cresthaven. No wind rattled the chimes, no snow fell, just crystalline sunlight pouring through the skylights like the universe had finally decided to play nice and give them one calm day before the grand finale.

The family gathered in the foyer, bleary-eyed but buzzing from yesterday's therapy breakthrough and the lingering afterglow of shared tears, laughter, and the realization that Elias had been trying to heal them all along—even from beyond.

Clara held the journal open to the newest page, discovered tucked behind the mechanical heart's final valve like a cardiac Easter egg wrapped in enigma.

"One more clue," she said, voice steady but thick with anticipation. "He saved the snarkiest—and sweetest—for last."

She read:

"Leonardo's codices held his secrets in reverse. Find where I wrote my final equation—the one that balances art, invention, and love. The door opens only when the family stands in proportion. (Hint: not da Vinci's. Yours. And Mona's been waiting patiently.)"

Julian snapped his fingers with theatrical flair, nearly knocking over a vase. "The Codex Closet! West wing—he called it that because he wrote mirror-script like da Vinci during his manic phases. Said it kept the 'mundane minds' from stealing his brilliance. And Mona? Father's missing sixth Mona Lisa! He hid it during his last low—said 'She knows too much to be seen yet.'"

Bea snorted, clutching her coffee like a lifeline. "Mundane minds like the IRS? Or the fire department after the 'perpetual motion barbecue' that nearly took out the carriage house?"

Theo grinned, phone finally pocketed (a minor miracle). "Chat would pay top dollar for the missing Mona reveal. 'Mona Voss: The Final Smile.' They're already theorizing alien involvement, thanks to Dad's old rants."

Lila rolled her eyes. "Because nothing says closure like turning Grandpa's masterpiece into a conspiracy thread."

Milo bounced ahead, duffel clanking. "Race you to the closet! The loser has to explain the missing Mona to the art critics tomorrow!"

Harper skipped behind, wind chimes jingling like an excited soundtrack. "The chimes say Mona's been lonely. She wants to come home!"

Clara led the parade down the west wing hallway, which ended at an unassuming door painted the exact shade of the house's exterior—camouflaged genius at its best.

The door featured no handle, only an engraved brass plate with da Vinci-style mirror writing and sliding tiles depicting the Vitruvian Man in pieces —head, torso, arms, legs—each movable.

Below, reverse script: "Arrange us as we truly are—imperfect, fabulous, and late to everything. Mona approves."

Julian struck a pose. "Obviously, my arms go in the 'dramatic flourish' position. Father always said my gestures were 'Renaissance-level extra.'"

Bea shoved him aside playfully. "Obviously, my torso goes in the 'actually holding this family together' slot. You'd collapse without my structural integrity."

Theo: "I call the head—because I'm always filming from behind the lens, never in the picture. Classic observer syndrome."

Lila: "Dibs on the legs. I'm the one running from all your drama—and toward the snacks." Milo: "I'll take the gears—wait, there are no gears. Rude. Dad's trolling us from the grave."

Harper: "I get the heart! Because I'm the cute one. And Mona's smile is heart-shaped!"

Clara: "Children. Focus. Or we'll be here until the next ice age, and Mona will die of boredom."

They rearranged the tiles—arguing, laughing, shoving, with running commentary.

Attempt One: Perfect da Vinci proportions.
Nothing.
Julian: "Father's trolling us from the grave. Classic. He always said perfection was overrated."

Attempt Two: Julian's dramatic arm span, Bea's squared shoulders, Theo's slouch.

Click.

The door swung inward.

Julian bowed theatrically. "Thank you, thank you. My proportions save the day—again."
Bea: "Your proportions are 90% ego, 10% hot air. But I'll allow it—this time."

Theo: "And 100% accurate, apparently. Dad knew us better than we know ourselves."

The Codex Closet was intimate—a cozy, book-lined nook with a single skylight casting golden beams on dust motes dancing like tiny Vitruvian figures.

Shelves groaned with leather-bound codices in mirror-script: inventions, sketches, equations blending art and science.
In the center, on a pedestal: the final codex, bound in deep blue leather, titled "Familia."

They opened it together—carefully, reverently, hands overlapping.
Pages of breathtaking work: anatomical hearts intertwined with family portraits, ornithopter wings on grandkids' backs, Vitruvian figures holding hands in infinite circles.

And the last page—an equation in Elias's hand:

$G = A + I + L^2$
Where G = Genius

A = Art

I = Invention

L = Love (squared, because it multiplies everything)

Below, his note—regular script for once:

"I spent my life chasing A and I, convinced they defined me. But the equation was incomplete without L. Bipolar highs gave me wings; lows showed me gravity. You—my flawed, brilliant, argumentative, paint-splattered family—supplied the love that kept me flying without crashing forever.
The house, the works, the riddles—they're yours to share or safeguard as you see fit. But the real legacy isn't hidden in walls. It's walking around, bickering, laughing, forgiving.
I got it wrong for years. Genius isn't solitary. It's collaborative. You are my greatest collaboration.
Thank you for finishing me.
All my love, squared and beyond—Elias."

Silence—thick, emotional.

Julian's voice cracked first, trying for wit. "He… he squared love because it grows exponentially. Dad doing math puns from the grave—ruthless. And accurate."

Bea laughed through tears. "He called us flawed and brilliant in the same sentence. Typical passive-aggressive genius. 'I love you but fix your proportions.'"

Theo wiped his eyes, grinning. "He knew we'd fight over the equation. Then realize we're the variables—and the answer."

Lila: "He made us the solution. Sneaky old man. With perfect emotional algebra."

Milo spun an imaginary gear. "And the missing tooth was always us—holding it together." Harper hugged the codex. "Grandpa's not unfinished anymore. He's… solved."

Clara closed it gently—then noticed a thin cord attached to the back cover, leading to a hidden panel in the closet wall.

She tugged.
A soft whirr.

The back wall slid aside, revealing a small, velvet-lined alcove.
Inside: the missing sixth Mona Lisa.

But not da Vinci's.

Elias's final version: Mona Lisa's face, but with subtle, heartbreaking differences. The smile was his own—enigmatic, knowing, tinged with the sadness of his lows and the joy of his highs. The background: the Voss house, the family in tiny Vitruvian poses, holding hands. And in Mona's eyes—reflections of each family member, looking back with love.

A plaque beneath:

"Mona Voss: The Smile That Stayed

She watched me through every storm.

She knew my secrets, my failures, my joys.

She never judged.

She just smiled—and waited for you to see her too.

This is the only Mona I ever truly painted.

The one who saw me.

The one who saw us.

Thank you for finding her.

—E"

The room fell silent again—this time, reverent. Julian's voice was barely a whisper. "He painted himself as her. The ultimate self-portrait."

Bea's tears fell freely. "And us in her eyes. We were always there."

Theo: "She's smiling because she knew we'd get here. Together."

Lila: "The knowing smile. Like 'Took you long enough.'"

Milo: "But worth the wait."

Harper pressed her face to the glass. "She's beautiful. And she's home."

Clara touched the canvas edge, voice trembling but strong.
"He was wrong about one thing," she said. "He didn't need finishing. He just needed us to catch up. And Mona—she was waiting to tell us that."

Julian pulled her into a hug. "We overlapped pretty spectacularly this week." Bea joined. "Even with chocolate, paint, exploding hearts, and therapy."
Theo: "And no more filming the sacred stuff. Promise."

Lila: "Mostly."
Milo: "Scout's honor."
Harper: "The chimes approve. They're singing the Mona song now."
They stood there—paint remnants, tear tracks, laughter bubbling up.

Julian raised an imaginary glass. "To Dad—the ultimate escape artist. Pulled off the greatest disappearing act, then left the best breadcrumb trail ever."

Bea: "And to Mom—for not murdering us when we turned his house into a disaster movie."

Clara: "Don't tempt me. There's still tomorrow's public unveiling."

Theo: "Chat's gonna lose their minds when they see Mona Voss."

Julian: "Let them. For once, it's not about views. It's about us."

Outside, the wind finally stirred—gentle, carrying the faint jingle of chimes in perfect, smiling harmony.

Tomorrow's unveiling would be grand.

But the real one—the equation solved, Mona found, love squared—was already complete.

Chapter 8: The Auction Ambush, the Great Easel Escape, and the Grand Unveiling

Saturday—the official grand finale of Leonardo's Legacy Weekend—arrived as if the universe had hired a full orchestra, a fireworks crew, and a mischievous god for special effects. The sun blazed in a clear Colorado sky, the air crisp with pine and excitement, and the Voss estate looked like a mix between an art museum and a county fair on steroids.

By noon, the grounds buzzed with activity: valets grappling with Teslas and Subarus alike, caterers balancing trays of gluten-free, dairy-free, joy-free canapés (now with extra caution after yesterday's torte incident), and the string quartet—battle-hardened veterans of pink paint, bodily fluids, and chocolate warfare—playing Vivaldi with the grim determination of soldiers who'd survived multiple tours and were ready for anything.

Clara stood at the entrance like a general inspecting troops, clipboard in one hand, coffee in the other. "Rule reminder: look, don't buy. Admire, don't acquire. And if Valentina Crowe shows up, smile sweetly and point her to the exit—preferably with a security escort."

Julian, wearing a fresh velvet blazer ("minimalist mourning chic, phase two"), adjusted a spotlight with the focus of a Broadway director. "Mother, the heart model needs chiaroscuro! It's begging for Renaissance drama! The valves must cast shadows that whisper 'genius at work.'"

Bea, clipboard welded to her hand like an extension of her arm, snapped, "The only thing begging is my sanity. One fingerprint on the biomimetic pump and I'll sue them into the Stone Age. Or at least the Renaissance."

Theo, finally filming with artistic flair instead of viral panic, murmured into his mic, "Chat's calling this 'Voss vs. Vultures: The Final Showdown.' They're ready for blood—or at least more frosting. Donations are pouring in for 'whatever chaos happens next.'"

Lila and Milo unveiled the grandkids' collaborative sculpture with a flourish—a chaotic whirl of gears, wings, hearts, and now a tiny Mona Lisa smile etched into a central cog. Harper hung her wind chimes overhead like a spiritual mobile. "Spirit commentary track engaged! Mona's watching!"

Clara exhaled, surveying the ballroom transformed into an elegant exhibit: carefully chosen pieces from the week's discoveries—the ornithopter wings hanging like a chandelier, the mechanical heart gently pulsing under glass, the Vitruvian family painting shining under soft lights, and the storm mural from the shelter taking center stage.

"No explosions today," she declared. "I'm speaking it into existence. Positive manifestation only."

The universe, as usual, took that as a dare.
The doors opened at 1 p.m. sharp. A tidal wave of berets, linen, Patagonia vests, and oversized egos poured in—local patrons, Denver collectors, New York scouts who'd jetted in after Theo's clips hit forty million, and even a few international art bloggers live-streaming in multiple languages.

Valentina Crowe arrived fashionably late, gliding in like a shark wearing Louboutins and a smile sharp enough to cut glass. Assistants trailed with iPads and iced matcha lattes that screamed "I summer in the Hamptons."

She air-kissed Clara with sniper precision. "Clara, darling, what a triumph. I simply must secure exclusive rights. Elias's late works are screaming 'Sotheby's'—or at least my gallery's white walls and 50% commission."

Clara's smile could freeze vodka. "They're screaming 'foundation only.' Loudly. And permanently."

Valentina's eyes sparkled like a predator sensing weakness. "Everything has a price, darling. Especially genius this... untamed. I have a collector on speed-dial offering five million for the heart alone. Cash. Today."

Julian swooped in, blazer gleaming. "Untamed? Madam, this is curated chaos! Refined revelation! Not a clearance rack at Art Basel!"
Valentina patted his cheek like a condescending aunt. "Sweetie, leave the commerce to the grown-ups. Your job is to look brooding in the catalog

photos. Preferably without chocolate in your hair this time."

Bea materialized, voice razor-sharp. "The grown-ups have voted. Unanimously. No deal. And if you touch one piece, I'll have you escorted out faster than you can say 'commission cut.'"

Valentina leaned in, voice dripping honeyed venom. "I have ways of persuading reluctant sellers. Watch and learn."

Theo whispered to the camera, "And there's the bait. Chat's screaming 'trap!' Donations spiking for 'Valentina takedown round two.'"

Valentina, undeterred, announced an "impromptu appraisal session" in the sunroom and—through means that definitely involved bribery, distraction, and assistant sleight of hand—had already moved three smaller pieces onto easels under portable spotlights while the family was greeting early guests.

The family charged in like the Avengers after the wrong Infinity Stone—Julian leading with dramatic cape swirl (he'd snuck one in after all), Bea brandishing her clipboard like a sword, Theo filming with glee.

Valentina stood at a velvet-draped podium, gavel raised (seriously—where did she get a gavel? eBay overnight? Bribery of a local judge?). "Lot one: 'Vitruvian Heartbeat.' Bidding opens at fifty thousand!"

Tech Bro in Patagonia vest: "Seventy-five! It's interactive genius!"
Valentina: "Seventy-five! Do I hear—"
Julian: "You hear grand larceny! That's artistic kidnapping with a side of extortion!"

Bea: "I'm speed-dialing the sheriff, my litigation team, and possibly the FBI art crimes division!" Theo: "Chat says make it pay-per-view. I'm inclined to agree—donations just hit ten grand for 'live justice.'"

The center easel—holding the delicate "Vitruvian Heartbeat" canvas with embedded clockwork—began to thrum ominously.

Valentina, oblivious: "One hundred thousand!" Canvas pulsed faster, gears whirring like an angry hornet.
Tech Bro: "It's alive! One-fifty! I need this for my startup lobby!"

Julian lunged to steady it. "Don't encourage the mechanism, you capitalist hyena! It's sensitive!" Bea grabbed the other side. "Stop bidding on my father's literal heartbeat, you vulture in venture capital clothing!" Bea yelled, clipboard clattering as she pointed accusingly at the Tech Bro. The tension snapped; Julian lunged for the easel, Bea grabbed his cape, and the crowd's gasps grew louder as Theo's livestream chat exploded in all-caps. The room pulsed with a frenzy of raised paddles and frantic keystrokes, Valentina's gavel knocked askew by the chaos. The canvas trembled, gears rattled, as if the art itself was protesting the spectacle—setting the stage for the upcoming tug-of-war that would send pastries flying and reputations spiraling into a swirl of ganache and glory.

Tug-of-war started—Julian pulling one way, Bea the other, Tech Bro waving his paddle like a surrender flag in reverse.

Theo: "This is better than Netflix. And the subscription's free chaos. Chat's crashing from excitement."

The easel legs—hastily assembled by Valentina's trembling assistants who were now regretting their life choices—buckled with a comedic crack. Valentina: "Going once—"

The canvas launched like a medieval siege weapon engineered by a very petty genius, arcing majestically over the crowd in slow-motion glory—straight toward the seven-layer chocolate torte on the dessert table.

Impact: splat.

Frosting detonated in a glorious brown mushroom cloud that would make Hiroshima jealous and pastry chefs weep.
Valentina emerged looking like the victim of the world's most expensive mud wrestle—face smeared, hair a chocolate helmet, Louboutins squelching.

She shrieked: "This is assault! By ganache! I'll sue for emotional distress and dry-cleaning!"

Tech Bro, dripping ganache like a melted statue, raised a frosting-coated paddle. "I'll take the cake painting! Two hundred K! It's immersive! Experiential! NFT potential!"

Julian, licking chocolate off his sleeve with dignity that shouldn't exist in such circumstances: "Father's final review of the art market: 'Needs more flavor. And fewer vultures.'" Bea, trying not to laugh and failing spectacularly: "You're wearing the evidence, Valentina. Literally. The canvas is now 'Chocolate Vitruvian'—limited edition."

Clara stepped forward, frosting in her hair like a crown of victory. "Leave. Now. Before the next course is the tiramisu trebuchet—or I call the sheriff and let him explain 'trespass with chocolate intent.'"

Valentina stormed out, assistants slipping on ganache like it was banana-peel ballet, one face-planting into a tray of éclairs for good measure. The crowd—half horrified, half mesmerized—burst into applause that rattled the chandeliers.

Someone yelled, "Eleven out of ten! Would attend again!"

Another: "Best performance art since Marina Abramović met Willy Wonka!"

A third: "I came for genius—I stayed for dessert warfare!"

Harper's chimes jingled wildly from the doorway, as if Elias were doubled over laughing in the afterlife, wiping tears with Mona Lisa's enigmatic sleeve.

Clara turned to the wreckage—easels toppled, sketches askew, chocolate everywhere like a crime scene at a bakery—then to her family: paint remnants, frosting war paint, and utter triumph. "Cleanup on aisle genius," she deadpanned, voice carrying over the laughter. "Then we reopen the real show. No vultures, no gavels, no unsolicited bidding wars."

Julian raised a chocolate-covered fist like a revolutionary. "To Dad—the ultimate escape artist! Turned an ambush into a dessert ambush. Genius!"

Bea: "And to Mom—for not murdering anyone. Yet. Though Valentina's on probation."

Theo: "Chat's at fifty million views. We broke the internet—again. Donations just funded the foundation for a year."

Lila high-fived Milo through the mess. "Grandpa: four. Vulture: zero. And counting."

Harper: "The chimes say it's the sweetest victory ever! Literally!"

They dove into cleanup—mopping, laughing, licking frosting off priceless sketches like kids at a forbidden party, guests joining in with napkins and enthusiasm.

The ambush had flopped spectacularly.
But the public unveiling?
It was just beginning.

With the sunroom cleared and the "Chocolate Vitruvian" carefully preserved as an accidental masterpiece, Clara reopened the ballroom doors at 3 p.m. to a growing crowd—news of the "frosting incident" spreading rapidly on social media.

The real exhibit shone: the ornithopter wings suspended like a chandelier of dreams, the mechanical heart pulsing gently under glass, the storm mural glowing with inner thunder, the family Vitruvian painting radiating connection, and—center stage—the newly revealed Mona Voss, unveiled with quiet ceremony.

The crowd hushed as Clara spoke—no microphone needed, her voice carrying the weight of love and loss.

"Your father—Elias Voss—wasn't just a genius. He was a man. Flawed. Brilliant. Stormy. Loving. These works aren't for sale. They're for sharing. For remembering that genius isn't perfect. It's human."

She gestured to Mona Voss—Elias's self-portrait smile, the family in her eyes. "This is his final smile. The one that saw everything—and loved us anyway."

Applause thundered—genuine, moved.

Julian stepped forward, voice thick. "He squared love in his equation. Because it multiplies. We're proof."

Bea: "The foundation launches today. Scholarships for art, invention, and mental health. Because genius needs support—not just spotlights."
Theo turned the camera to the crowd for once. "This isn't content. It's legacy."

Guests lingered—tears, laughter, donations pouring in. Children touched the ornithopter wings in awe. Couples held hands in front of the storm mural. An elderly woman whispered to Clara, "My husband was like him. Thank you for showing the whole picture."

As evening fell, the family gathered on the porch—exhausted, triumphant, whole.

Julian raised a glass of champagne (non-exploding variety). "To Dad—the man who turned chaos into connection."

Bea: "And to us—for surviving it with style."

Theo: "And chocolate."

Lila: "And love. Squared."

Milo: "Exponential."

Harper: "Infinite."

Clara looked at the stars emerging. "He got his wish. We finished him—together."

The wind chimes sang—Mona's smile in sound.

The weekend ended not with a bang, but with a perfect, quiet harmony.

The legacy wasn't the works on the walls.

It was the family standing together—imperfect, infinite, smiling.

The End

======

Epilogue: The Voss Collective – One Year Later

October in Cresthaven always smelled like turning leaves and fresh possibility. The Voss house looked much the same from the outside—eccentric Victorian, turrets winking in the sun—but inside, everything had changed.

The Voss Collective had opened its doors six months earlier: a nonprofit foundation born from Elias's legacy and the family's hard-won unity. The house itself was now part gallery, part workshop, and part community center.

Visitors came from across the country—some for the art, some for the inventions, many for the story of a family that turned private chaos into public healing.

The first major project—launched exactly one year after Leonardo's Legacy Weekend—was called **"The Unfinished Project."**

It started with an idea Clara proposed the week after the finale: invite aspiring artists, inventors, and anyone affected by mental health struggles to submit unfinished work—paintings, gadgets, poems, songs, or anything halted by doubt, illness, or life's storms.

The Collective would match submissions with mentors—sometimes the Voss family themselves, other times professionals—and assist in finishing them collaboratively. No deadlines. No judgment. Just completion, in whatever form it took.

The inaugural exhibition opened on the anniversary Saturday.

The ballroom—site of the notorious chocolate ambush—was changed again. Walls now showed finished pieces alongside their original unfinished states: a half-painted landscape now bursting with color added by a stranger who had known similar despair; a broken kinetic sculpture repaired and enhanced by Milo's steady hands; a poem about bipolar lows finished with verses from Julian's dramatic flair and Theo's quiet insight.

At the center: Elias's mechanical heart—restored, pulsing gently under glass—and beside it, Mona Voss, her enigmatic smile watching over everything.

The grandkids' area buzzed with kids: Harper leading a wind-chime workshop, teaching children to "listen for the smiles in the breeze." Lila mentored young painters struggling with perfectionism. Milo ran a gadget lab where teens fixed broken dreams into working realities.

Julian—now teaching dramatic performance for "expressive vulnerability"—led a group in theatrical readings of unfinished plays, turning stilted dialogue into cathartic comedy.

Bea handled the legal aspects—scholarships, grants, and pro bono assistance for artists accessing mental health resources. She traded some billable hours for something more meaningful.

Theo's documentary—The Unfinished Masterpieces—premiered that night. No viral stunts. Just honest footage: the chaos, the tears, the laughter, the family learning to hold each other's umbrellas.

Clara stood on the porch at dusk, watching visitors leave with new works in hand, faces lighter. Julian joined her, no cape today—just a simple sweater. "We did it, Mom. His equation works."

Bea, arm linked with Theo's: "Love squared. Exponential growth. The numbers finally make sense." Theo: "And no ring light required."
Lila and Milo carried trays of cupcakes—chocolate, of course—with tiny fondant Mona smiles.

Harper ran up, wind chimes jingling. "Mona says the project's a masterpiece!"

Clara looked at the houselights glowing, laughter spilling out, unfinished lives becoming whole.

"Your father," she said softly, "would call this sentimental sabotage."

Julian smiled. "Then invent a tear-powered generator to harness it."

Bea: "Patent pending—by all of us."

They stood together—imperfect proportions, infinite love.

The wind chimes sang Mona's smile.

And Elias's greatest masterpiece endured—not in hidden studios or perfect equations, but in the messy, collaborative, constantly evolving beauty of family.

The End

(For real this time.)

Made in the USA
Coppell, TX
20 January 2026

68879952R00069